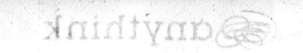

JUST KIDDING!

JOKES AND More

About Fish

By Maria Nelson

Gareth Stevens
PUBLISHING

Please visit our website, www.garethstevens.com. For a free color catalog of all our high-quality books, call toll free 1-800-542-2595 or fax 1-877-542-2596.

Library of Congress Cataloging-in-Publication Data

Nelson, Maria.
Jokes and more about fish / by Maria Nelson.
    p. cm. — (Just kidding!)
Includes index.
ISBN 978-1-4824-0546-0 (pbk.)
ISBN 978-1-4824-3323-4 (6-pack)
ISBN 978-1-4824-0547-7 (library binding)
1. Wit and humor, Juvenile. 2. Fishes — Juvenile humor. I. Nelson, Maria. II. Title.
PN6163.N45 2014
818—dc23

Published in 2015 by
Gareth Stevens Publishing
111 East 14th Street, Suite 349
New York, NY 10003

Designer: Sarah Liddell
Editor: Kristen Rajczak

Photo credits: Cover, p. 1 Eric Isselee/Shutterstock.com; p. 5 hxdbzxy/Shutterstock.com; pp. 6, 9, 10, 13, 14, 17, 18 Memo Angeles/Shutterstock.com; pp. 7, 8 bluehand/Shutterstock.com; pp. 11, 22 (bottom fish) Kletr/Shutterstock.com; pp. 12, 19 holbox/Shutterstock.com; p. 15 Havoc/Shutterstock.com; p. 16 MaxkateUSA/Shutterstock.com; p. 20 ehtesham/Shutterstock.com; p. 21 xxuligan/Shutterstock.com; p. 22 (puffer fish) Judex/Shutterstock.com.

Printed in the United States of America

CPSIA compliance information: Batch #CS15GS: For further information contact Gareth Stevens, New York, New York at 1-800-542-2595.

Contents

Words in the glossary appear in **bold** type the first time they are used in the text.

More Than Swimmers

Have you ever seen a fish walk? Handfish have fins that look a lot like hands, and they use them to move along the bottom of the ocean. Flying fish have a **unique** shape that lets them burst out of the water and **glide** through the air.

Whether or not you giggle at the thought of fish doing anything more than swimming, fish are fun to joke about—especially because sharks, eels, and other sea creatures are officially fish, too!

Everyday Sayings

What did the fish say to his long-lost brother?
"Long time no sea!"

A salesman told the fish he could get a great deal.

The fish said, "What's the catch?"

What did the mother fish tell her brokenhearted son?
"Don't worry. There are plenty of fish in the sea."

Making Trouble

What did the fish say when he got out of jail?

"I'm off the hook!"

Money Matters

Name That Fish

What's the best-dressed fish in the ocean?

The swordfish. It always looks sharp.

What has big, sharp teeth, a tail, scales, and a trunk?
A pike going on vacation.

What kind of fish chases mice?
A catfish.

What kind of fish won't stop talking?

A big-mouthed bass.

Sharks!

What kind of shark can help you build a house?
A hammerhead.

Why wouldn't the shark attack the fish?

It had a lot of **mussels**.

What happened to the shark that swallowed a bunch of keys?
He got lockjaw.

14

What did the shark want to eat for its birthday?

A crab cake.

15

Don't Get Upset

Why did the goldfish hide in its bowl?

It felt like everyone was staring at it.

Why don't fish have computers?
They don't like to be caught online.

Why did the fish quit the game?
It was **floundering**.

What did the electric eel say after the movie?

"That ending was shocking."

Silly Stuff

What do you call a baby fish from France?
A French **fry**.

What part of a fish weighs the most?

Its scales.

If fish lived on land, which country would they live in?
Finland.

Gone Fishin'

What should you do if you want to talk to a fish?
Drop it a line.

What's a fisherman's favorite card game?
Go fish.

Fun and Funny Facts About Fish

Fish have great senses. They can see in color, and many have taste buds all over their body!

Most fish have an air **bladder** inside their bodies to keep them afloat. Sharks don't! They have to swim continuously, or they'll sink to the bottom.

Can you tell how old a fish is? Scientists can! They cut a piece off part of a fish's inner ear and count its rings—just like you would with a tree trunk!

Most fish lay eggs, but female sunfish are particularly impressive egg layers. They can each lay as many as 300 million eggs in one season!

The last place you'd expect to see a fish is on land. However, the African lungfish can live out of water for up to 2 years! It hides underground.

22

Glossary

anemone: a brightly colored sea animal that has tentacles and looks somewhat like a flower

artillery: large guns that shoot shells, bullets, or missiles

bladder: an expandable body part that holds air in fish

flounder: to struggle

fry: a baby fish

glide: to move in a smooth and graceful way

mussel: a small animal that lives in the water and has a shell

unique: one of a kind

For More Information

BOOKS

Gould, Francesca. *Why Fish Fart: Gross but True Things You'll Wish You Didn't Know.* New York, NY: G. P. Putnam's Sons, 2014.

Random House. *Funny-Side Up: A SpongeBob Joke Book.* New York, NY: Random House Books for Young Readers, 2014.

WEBSITES

EPA's Fish Kids Website
water.epa.gov/learn/kids/fishkids/index.cfm
Learn what fish are safe to eat, how to fish for food, and play games, too.

Videos: Fish
video.nationalgeographic.com/video/kids/fish-kids/
Watch lots of videos about different kinds of fish.